HISTORY & GEOGRAPHY

TROPICAL RAINFORESTS

Author:
Theresa K. Buskey, B.A., J.D.

Editor:
Alan Christopherson, M.S.

Assistant Editor:
Annette M. Walker, B.S.

Media Credits:
Page 3: © odmeyer, iStock, Thinkstock; **4:** © Frederic Prochasson, iStock, Thinkstock; **9:** © Richard Orr, Dorling Kindersley, Thinkstock; **12:** © Ameng Wu, iStock, Thinkstock, © Eric Isselée, iStock, Thinkstock; **13:** © Omar Ariff, iStock, Thinkstock; © Ammit, iStock, Thinkstock; **14:** © Nelson A. Ishikawa, iStock, Thinkstock; **16:** © kviktor01, iStock, Thinkstock; **22:** © estivillml, iStock, Thinkstock; **26:** © Sohadiszno, iStock, Thinkstock, © Dorling Kindersley, Thinkstock; **28:** © lzf, iStock, Thinkstock; **30:** © Judy Dillon, iStock, Thinkstock; **32:** © atosan, iStock, Thinkstock; **34:** © walking onstreet, iStock, Thinkstock; **40:** © Alejandro Palacio, iStock, Thinkstock; **42:** © Robert Ford, iStock, Thinkstock; **44:** © Anke Van wyk, Hemera, Thinkstock; **45:** © Dave Barfield, iStock, Thinkstock; **46:** © Photos.com, Thinkstock; **51:** © Peter Visscher, Dorling Kindersley, Thinkstock; **53:** © Natasha Chamberlain, Dorling Kindersley, Thinkstock.

Alpha Omega
PUBLICATIONS

804 N. 2nd Ave. E.
Rock Rapids, IA 51246-1759

TROPICAL RAINFORESTS

In this **LIFEPAC®** you will learn about huge, warm forests on the earth where rain falls almost every day. You will discover what these forests are like. You will also learn about the animals and people who live there. You will learn how the things that grow in the forests are used today and why the forests are getting smaller.

Objectives

Read these objectives. The objectives tell you what you will be able to do when you have successfully completed this LIFEPAC. Each section will list according to the numbers below what objectives will be met in that section. When you have finished this LIFEPAC, you should be able to:

1. Describe rainforests and tell where they are located.
2. Name some of the products of the rainforest.
3. Identify some of the rainforest plants and animals.
4. Explain the history of the Amazon and Congo rainforests.
5. Describe the Congo and Amazon Rivers.
6. Tell of the changes being made in the rainforest.
7. Describe how people live in the rainforest.

1. RAINFORESTS OF THE WORLD

A rainforest is also known as a jungle. It is a thick forest that grows in the region known as the tropics. These forests are very warm and get lots of rain. Many, many, many kinds of plants, animals, and insects live in rainforests. You will learn about only a few of them.

Objectives

Review these objectives. When you have completed this section, you should be able to:

1. Describe rainforests and tell where they are located.
2. Name some of the products of the rainforest.
3. Identify some of the rainforest plants and animals.
6. Tell of the changes being made in the rainforest.
7. Describe how people live in the rainforest.

Vocabulary

Study these new words. Learning the meanings of these words is a good study habit and will improve your understanding of this LIFEPAC.

abundant (ə bun′ dənt). More than enough; very plentiful.

balsa (bôl′ sə). A tree with very lightweight wood.

basin (bā′ sən). The land area drained by a river and the streams that flow into the river.

classify (klas′ i fī). To arrange in groups or classes.

hothouse (hot′ hous). A building with a glass roof and sides, kept warm for growing plants.

humid (hyü′ mid). Damp or moist air.

Latin America (Lat′ n ə mer′ə ka). South America, Central America Mexico, and most of the West Indies.

mahogany (mə hog' ə nē). A tropical tree that has dark reddish-brown wood. It polishes very well and is used to make furniture.

nutrient (nü' trē ənt). Any substance that is needed by living things for energy, growth, and repair of injuries.

salamander (sal' ə man dər). An animal shaped like a lizard, but belonging to the same group as frogs and toads.

settler (set' ler). A person who goes to live in a new country or area.

species (spē' shēz). A group of related living things that have certain important parts or features in common.

steward (stü' ərd). A person who takes care of or manages the property of someone else. (The earth belongs to God and we take care of it for Him).

teak (tēk). A tall tropical tree with hard, heavy, durable wood used for furniture and shipbuilding.

temperate zone (tem' pər it zōn). Area of the earth in between the hot tropics and the cold arctic. Most of the USA is in the temperate zone.

tropics (trop' iks). Regions near the equator, between the Tropic of Cancer and the Tropic of Capricorn.

Note: *All vocabulary words in this LIFEPAC appear in* **boldface** *print the first time they are used. If you are unsure of the meaning when you are reading, study the definitions given.*

Pronunciation Key: hat, āge, cãre, fär; let, ēqual, tėrm; it, īce; hot, ōpen, ôrder; oil; out; cup, pu̇t, rüle; child; long; thin; /ℱH/ for **th**en; /zh/ for mea**s**ure; /u/ or /ə/ represents /a/ in **a**bout, /e/ in tak**e**n, /i/ in penc**i**l, /o/ in lem**o**n, and /u/ in circ**u**s.

Facts about Rainforests

A rainforest, or jungle, can only grow when the temperature and the rainfall are just right. The temperature must be around 80° all year. It can not get much hotter or cooler than that. The forest has to get at least 80 inches of rain in a year, and that rain must fall regularly all year. Some rainforests get 200-300 inches of rain in a year! (Remember, deserts get only 10 inches or less in a year). This makes the forest very green with many kinds of life in it.

Rainforests usually grow near the equator. That is the best place to find the hot temperatures and regular rainfall needed for a rainforest. The area around the equator between the Tropic of Cancer and the Tropic of Capricorn is where most rainforests grow. This is called the tropics, and the jungles there are often called tropical rainforests.

Cold arctic air cannot hold much moisture, but the hot air of the tropics can carry large amounts of water. Rainforests occur all along the equator when the rain is not blocked by mountains or cooler air.

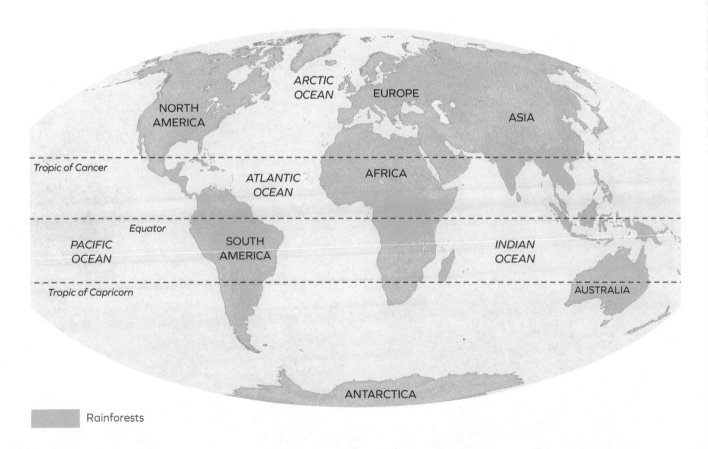

Rainforests

| Major Rainforests of the World. This map is also for questions 1.1 to 1.4.

There are three main areas of tropical rainforest in the world. They are in **Latin America**, Africa, and Southeast Asia. Each area has animals and plants that the others do not have. But, the types of plants and animals are very much alike in all of the rainforests.

Latin America has more rainforests than the other regions. The rainforest that covers the **basin** of the Amazon River in Brazil, South America is the largest in the world. It covers one-third of South America. Other rainforests also cover much of Central America and strips along the east coast of South America.

The second largest total area of rainforest is in southern Asia. It covers mainly the peninsulas of southeast Asia and the islands heading south to Australia. The countries of that region, Indonesia, Malaysia, Thailand, the Philippines, Vietnam, Kampuchea, and Myanmar are mostly rainforest.

The last area of rainforest is in Africa. It covers the center of the continent around the equator and includes a part of the large island of Madagascar on Africa's east coast. The largest rainforest of Africa is in the Congo River Basin, mostly in the country of the Democratic Republic of the Congo.

Map exercises.

1.1   Using a pencil, lightly shade in the area on the map called the tropics.

1.2   Put a box around the largest region of rainforest in the world.

1.3   Circle the rainforests of Southeast Asia.

1.4   Put an *X* on the island of Madagascar.

Complete the sentences.

1.5   The three regions of rainforest are in _____ , _____ , and _____ .

1.6   The largest rainforest in the world is in the basin of the _____ _____ .

1.7   Rainforests usually grow near the _____ .

1.8   Rainforests need _____ temperatures and _____ rainfall.

1.9   A rainforest gets at least _____ inches of rain in a year.

Rainforests are like huge **hothouses**. Thousands of different kinds of plants live there. A small part of a rainforest that covers 2 ½ acres may have over a hundred different kinds of trees! That is unusual because the same size piece of forest which is in the United States, in the **temperate zone**, may have at most seven kinds of trees.

The rainforest is always green. Some trees do lose their leaves for a short time, but the forest never becomes bare like a temperate forest in the winter. It never gets cold enough to kill off insects or plants, as it does in the temperate and arctic regions. There are flowers blooming and fruit ripening year round in the rainforests. That means there is always a good supply of food for animals. A constant supply of many kinds of food means that many kinds of animals can live in the rainforest.

About half of all of the different kinds, or **species**, of plants and animals in the entire world live in the rainforests. Many of the plants, animals, and insects do not even have names. They have never been **classified** by a scientist.

When a scientist finds a new animal or plant, he classifies it by deciding what group, or class, it is similar to. Then, he gives it a name in Latin, which is the language of scientific names. Like an explorer who finds new land, he can give it any name he wants. Often newly-found animals or plants are named after the person who classified them. Scientists are always finding new species in the rainforests.

Rainforests are very complicated places. Scientists think of the rainforest in three layers. The top layer is the *canopy*. The canopy is the tallest trees that grow to be 75-150 feet tall. Under the tall canopy is the *understory*. The understory is made up of smaller trees, vines, and shrubs. The bottom layer is the forest *floor*. This is made up of the small plants on the ground.

The canopy is like a huge green roof over the forest. The trees grow up thin and straight, like pillars. They do not put out branches until they are very tall. Then, they spread out like an umbrella in the sunlight. The trees are so close together that very little light or rain goes through to the lower layers.

Many kinds of monkeys, birds, and insects live in the canopy. These kinds of animals often never touch the ground in their entire life! All the food and water they need, they find among the tall trees. Because it rains all the time, water can be found in holes in the trees, leaves, and plants that grow on the trees. The animals eat the leaves and fruit of the trees, insects, or other animals.

The understory is usually a dark, **humid** place. There is very little light and no breeze because they are blocked out by the canopy. The plants under the canopy must be able to live with very little sunlight. Often they will only grow in open patches where a big tree has fallen down. Other plants, like vines, grow on the big trees. They get the **nutrients** they need from the tree, which is getting sunlight up in the canopy.

The floor of the rainforest is often very open and easy to walk across. That is because so little light reaches the floor, very few plants can grow there. The movies are wrong in showing people cutting their way through the thick plants and vines in the jungle. That type of jungle is only found around rivers and clearings, where light can reach the forest floor.

| Levels of the rainforest canopy

People from Europe, who first explored rain forests, thought the soil there had to be very rich in nutrients because the forest is so green and thick. They expected to be able to grow many kinds of crops and trees if they cleared the land, but they were very wrong.

In fact, the soil in a rain forest is very poor. Things are lush and green only because they get a constant supply of nutrients from the plants and animals that die and fall to the forest floor. On the floor, many special plants and insects break up this natural "trash" and recycle it into the soil. There it is quickly absorbed by the plants and used again.

Any nutrients that do get into the soil are washed away by all the rain. If the forest is cut down, the supply of new nutrients stops. The soil quickly runs out of nutrients and within a few years nothing will grow in it.

Some of the rain in a rain forest is also recycled. The trees put the water back into the air through small holes in their leaves. This makes the air more humid and causes it to rain again. That creates a steady supply of rain for the forest and the rivers that flow through it. As much as half the rain in the Amazon may come from the forest itself! In places where the forest has been cut down, less rain falls.

Match the following.

1.10 _____ canopy

1.11 _____ understory

1.12 _____ floor

1.13 _____ nutrients

1.14 _____ classify

a. putting something in a group with others like it

b. top of the tallest rainforest trees

c. ground level of the rainforest

d. needed by living things to grow

e. middle level of the rainforest

Complete the sentences.

1.15 The soil in the rainforest is very _____ .

1.16 Rainforests do not become bare like those in the _____ _____ .

1.17 A rainforest has _____ kinds of plants.

1.18 About half of the _____ of animals in the world live in the rainforest.

1.19 Few plants can grow on the forest floor because very little _____ reaches there.

Answer these questions.

1.20   Where do the rainforest plants get their nutrients?

_____

_____

1.21   How is rain recycled in the rainforest?

_____

_____

Plants and Animals

God created a huge variety of plants and animals to live in the rainforest. Many of them need each other to survive. All of them were specially made to live in the hot, wet forests.

The tall canopy trees must be able to reach the sunlight high in the air and still get nutrients from the thin soil on the forest floor. Their roots do not go deep into the soil because there is nothing there for the plants to reach. Instead the roots spread out in all directions along or just under the ground. That way they can quickly make use of the nutrients from the recycled plants and animals that have fallen to the floor.

One type of plant in the rainforest does not even need soil. These plants are called *epiphytes*, or air plants. Air plants live on the branches of other trees in the canopy or understory, with their roots out in the air. In the humid rainforest, they collect water from the rain that falls on them. They get nutrients from the natural "trash" that falls around them or from insects that make nests in their roots! One kind of air plant is a beautiful flower called an orchid. There are thousands of different kinds of orchids in the rainforest!

Some air plants store water in pools in and around their roots. These pools become homes for frogs and **salamanders**. Frogs usually need to lay their eggs in ponds, but some rainforest tree frogs lay their eggs in pools in the air plants. That way the frogs never have to go down to the ground.

Millions of kinds of insects live in the rainforest. It never gets cold enough to kill them. There are bees, butterflies, termites, beetles, and many kinds of flies. There are ants everywhere. One of the more interesting kinds of ants is the army ant. Army ants do not have nests. They march out in a line every day to hunt for other insects, which they eat. At night they hook themselves together to form a living nest around their queen and *larvae*, (lar' ve) or baby ants.

| Red-eyed Tree Frog

Snakes live in the trees and on the forest floor. They eat frogs, eggs, birds, insects, and small animals. Some of the snakes, like the fer de lance of Latin America, are poisonous, but others are not. One especially large non-poisonous snake is the anaconda of South America. It is one of the largest snakes in the world. A full-grown anaconda can be 30 feet long. The anaconda kills its prey by wrapping itself around the animal and squeezing it until it can not breathe. Then the snake swallows the prey whole. If the animal is big enough, the snake may not eat again for weeks!

| Blood Python

Monkeys are a very common animal in the rainforest. Most live all of their lives up in the canopy and the understory. God designed them to live among the trees. They have long arms to swing from branch to branch. Some can use their tails to hold onto the trees while they eat. They are very fast and agile (aj el), jumping easily from tree to tree as they search for food. Different monkeys eat different things. They can eat leaves, fruit, insects, eggs, nuts, flowers, roots, and frogs. Their hoots and howls are heard throughout the rainforest, even when they can not be seen among the trees.

Many colorful birds also live among the canopy of the rainforest. The most unusual are the Birds of Paradise from the forests of New Guinea and Australia. These birds are named for the

| Chimpanzee

unbelievably beautiful feathers on the male. The colors of their feathers vary from bright reds, to greens and blues. They often have long, unusual tail feathers that they display in a manner similar to a peacock. These birds were hunted for years for their feathers and are more difficult to find now.

There are also animals that live on the forest floor. The tapir is a forest animal that looks like a large pig. It is actually in the same animal family as the horse and the rhinoceros. They live in South American and Asian rainforests, eating leaves, twigs, and fruit.

Tapirs are only one of the animals hunted by the big cats of the rainforest. Jaguars, leopards, and tigers are the largest predators of the rainforest. All of these cats have beautiful fur coats that have made them desired by hunters for years. The spotted coats of the jaguar and leopard were especially popular for fur coats. Today most countries are trying to protect their big cats, but many are still hunted illegally.

These are only a very few of the animals and plants of the rainforest. The most important thing to remember is that there are so many different kinds of life there. You could study antelope, marmosets, parrots, moths, spiders, flowers, vines, or lizards and find dozens of kinds in the rainforest. The rainforest is where the plants and animals are the most **abundant**.

| Bird of Paradise

| A Tapir

Match the following.

1.22	_____	air plants
1.23	_____	monkeys
1.24	_____	anaconda
1.25	_____	army ants
1.26	_____	Birds of Paradise
1.27	_____	tapir
1.28	_____	jaguar
1.29	_____	tree frogs
1.30	_____	canopy trees

a. killed for their beautiful feathers

b. lay their eggs in pools in the canopy plants

c. form a living nest each night

d. related to the horse and rhinoceros

e. roots spread out along the ground

f. large predator, hunted for fur

g. fast, agile, live in the trees

h. live on the branches of trees, get nutrients from the air and rain

i. large snake, coils around its prey

People and the Rainforest

Traditional life. There are many tribes of people who have lived in the rainforests for thousands of years. These forest dwellers usually belong to one of two groups. They are usually hunter/gatherers or slash-and-burn farmers.

Hunter/gatherers live as they do in every other region of the world. They kill animals and gather what the forest provides for part of their food. Unlike in the Arctic, tools are always available. Unlike in the desert, water is always available. The people do

| Brazilian Indians

not need clothes to protect them from the weather. The forest even provides a way to make hunting easier. Many of the people hunt with poisoned arrows. The poisons come from the plants of the forest. That makes the animals easier to kill.

However, most of the forest people raise crops in small clearings as well as hunting and gathering in the forest. This provides them with food year-round. They start by cutting (slashing) down the trees and the other plants in an area. They let the dead plants dry out, then they burn them. The ash from the burned plants goes into the soil and makes it fertile for a little while. This is called slash-and-burn farming.

The small clearings grow food crops for a few years, then the family or group moves on and clears a new field. The old field is left to be over-grown by the forest. In a few years, it once again looks like the rainforest that surrounds it.

This type of farming does not harm the rainforest when only a few people are doing it. The small clearings become rainforest again without any damage. The land is used and recycled for use again some other time. The rainforest easily regrows to fill in the clearings after the people leave. That is changing today. Today, the rainforests are getting smaller because too many people are burning them.

 Complete the sentences.

1.31   The people of the rainforest traditionally lived as either _____
           _____ or _____ .

1.32   Many of the forest people hunt with _____ arrows.

1.33   The soil in a clearing is made fertile by _____ the dead plants.

1.34   After a clearing would no longer grow crops, it was left and soon became
           _____ .

Rainforests are in danger. There is a great deal of talk about the destruction of the rainforests today. It is a popular subject and a *fad*. That means, many people are writing, talking, and arguing about protecting the rainforests. Many of these people will find some new subject to get excited about when they get tired of rainforests, but people who love God should take care of the earth He gave us. We need to be good **stewards**. There are some serious problems concerning the rainforests that need to be fixed.

Rainforests are being cut down too quickly. Every year an area about the size of West Virginia is being destroyed. We will look at how this is happening and why it may be a problem for everyone.

Rainforests are so large and thick that for many years very few people lived or went there. Today, however, that is changing. Millions of poor, often hungry, people live near the rainforests of the world. These people are desperate for a better life, and they think they can find it in the forests.

Settlers can get into the rainforests because modern machines have opened roads deep into the jungle. The roads are

| Bulldozing roads into the forest

usually built by businesses who want to cut down trees or dig up minerals in the forest. Governments build other roads for trade and to allow settlers into the forest. Poor people come into the forest by the thousands on the roads and take land to raise food. They burn off the trees and plants to make a field. Then they plant crops for food and to sell. All around them other farmers do the same, so there is no forest left to grow back.

The new farms can only grow crops for a few years in the poor soil. The farmers then sell the land to a cattle rancher or just leave and clear a new piece of land. The soil is so poor that it will not even grow grass to feed cattle for more than a few more years. By then, the ground is hard packed and grows only a few weeds. The rainforest is destroyed and nothing can be done with the land.

Obviously, if this continues long enough, the forests will be destroyed and the farmers will have no place to move. Then those people will starve, because there will be no land left where they can grow food. Forcing them to stop cutting down the forest will not help, because they would just starve now instead of later. New ways need to be found for these people to live on the rainforest land without destroying it.

Also, no one knows how destroying the rainforests will change the earth. We know that less rain will fall once the trees are gone. That may cause some rivers, which supply water to cities around the rainforest, to dry up during part of the year. Also, burning trees puts *carbon* into the air. Carbon absorbs heat from the sun. Will the burning of so many trees change the air and make the climate on the earth warmer? Experts are arguing about it, but it might be happening.

The rainforests are also the source of many things that are useful to human beings. As many as one out of every four drugs bought at the store were discovered in a rainforest. Coffee, chocolate, bananas, corn, tea, sweet potatoes, Brazil nuts, rubber, and tapioca all came from the rainforest. Very valuable wood is taken from the trees of the rainforest. **Mahogany**, **teak**, and **balsa** wood come from there. Those trees can not be grown without the thick, wet, warm rainforests. Thus, the loss of the rainforests would hurt other people besides those that must live there.

God put people in charge of the earth. It is our job to use it wisely. Perhaps you will one day work to restore rainforests after they have been destroyed. You may even find new ways to feed the hungry people who are burning the forests. God has given us minds to find solutions to our problems with His help.

 Answer these questions.

1.35   How large of an area of rainforest is being destroyed each year?

_____

1.36   How do settlers get into the rainforest?

_____

1.37   What do the settlers do when their fields will not grow crops any more?

_____

_____

1.38   What two things might happen to the earth if the rainforests are burned?

a. _____

b. _____

1.39   Name six things we get from the rainforest.

_____

_____

 Do this activity.

1.40   Look over this list of rainforest plants and animals. Choose at least one name and look up information about it. Make a report for your class. Draw a picture to go with your report.

Animals		**Plants**	
anteater	macaw	balsa wood	curare
coati	manatee	Brazil nut tree	manioc
flamingo	toucan	cacao tree	orchids
iguana	vampire bat	cashew tree	quebracho tree
jaguar	sloth	cinchona tree	sassafras

✔ **Teacher check:**

Initials _____   Date _____

 Review the material in this section to prepare for the Self Test. The Self Test will check your understanding of this section. Any items you miss on this test will show you what areas you will need to restudy in order to prepare for the unit test.

SELF TEST 1

Match the following (3 points each answer).

1.01	_____ monkey	a. catch their water and nutrients from the air
1.02	_____ army ants	b. large snake
1.03	_____ tapir	c. looks like a large pig
1.04	_____ tree frog	d. beautifully colored feathers
1.05	_____ anaconda	e. tall, straight, pillar-like trunks
1.06	_____ Birds of Paradise	f. grow on trees and get nutrients from them
1.07	_____ orchids	g. always blooming and ripening
1.08	_____ canopy trees	h. make nests out of their bodies
1.09	_____ vines	i. agile, lives in the trees
1.010	_____ flowers and fruit	j. lay eggs in pools in the canopy

Answer these questions.

1.011 What two things must happen for a rainforest to grow? (4 points)

a. _____

b. _____

1.012 What are the three regions of rainforest in the world? (6 points)

a. _____

b. _____

c. _____

1.013 The soil of the rainforest gets nutrients from: (4 points)

_____

_____

_____

1.014 The people of the rainforest traditionally are either: (4 points)

a. _____

b. _____

1.015 How do farmers make the rainforest soil fertile for a short period of time?
(4 points)

_____

_____

Choose the correct word from the list below (3 points each answer).

canopy	understory	floor	tropics
equator	species	mahogany	roads
cattle ranches	drugs		

1.016 The mid-level of the rainforest, the area of small trees, vines, and shrubs, is
called the _____ .

1.017 As many as one out of four _____ from the store came from
the rainforest.

1.018 Most tropical rainforests are found near the map line called the
_____ .

1.019 The region between the Tropics of Cancer and Capricorn is called the
_____ .

1.020 The highest level of the rainforest, the tree tops, is called the
_____ .

1.021 About half of all of the _____ of plants and animals can be
found in the rainforests.

1.022 After the land cleared in the rainforest is no longer good for crops, it is often
used for _____ for a time.

1.023 The bottom level of the rainforest is the _____ .

1.024   Settlers get into the rainforest using _____ built by businesses and governments.

1.025   _____ is a valuable wood grown in the rainforest.

Answer *true* or *false* (2 points each answer).

1.026   _____   Every year an area of rainforest about the size of Europe is destroyed.

1.027   _____   Coffee, bananas, rubber, and tea come from the rainforests.

1.028   _____   Burning the rainforests might be making the earth warmer.

1.029   _____   The largest rainforest in the world is on the island of Madagascar.

1.030   _____   A forest in the temperate region will have more kinds of plants than a tropical rainforest.

1.031   _____   Trees in the rainforest give off moisture that is recycled and comes down again as rain.

1.032   _____   Many of the people of the rainforest hunt with poisoned arrows.

1.033   _____   After the rainforest has been burned, the land can be used for coffee and banana farms for many, many years.

1.034   _____   There is a large rainforest on the north side of Europe.

✔ **Teacher check:**

Score _____

Initials _____

Date _____

80 / 100

2. THE AMAZON RAINFOREST

The largest rainforest in the world is in the basin of the Amazon River of South America. It covers about one third of that continent. The rainforest touches all of the nations on the northern portion of South America.

You will learn about this huge jungle in this part of the LIFEPAC. You will learn about people who lived there in the past and how they used the land before the Europeans explored it. You will study the problems the people face today. Finally, you will learn a little about the animals of this forest.

Objectives

Review these objectives. When you have completed this section, you should be able to:

1. Describe rainforests and tell where they are located.
2. Name some of the products of the rainforest.
3. Identify some of the rainforest plants and animals.
4. Explain the history of the Amazon and Congo rainforests.
5. Describe the Congo and Amazon Rivers.
6. Tell of the changes being made in the rainforest.
7. Describe how people live in the rainforest.

Vocabulary

Study these new words. Learning the meanings of these words is a good study habit and will improve your understanding of this LIFEPAC.

anthropologist (an' thrə pol' ə jist). A person who studies the customs cultures, and beliefs of human beings.

boom (büm). A rapid growth.

dye (dī). Something that can be mixed with water and used to color cloth, hair, and other things.

ecotourism (e kō′ tur′ izm). Traveling to see endangered places or animals in the hopes that paying to see them will help protect them.

infamous (in′ fə məs). Well known for being bad.

latex (lā′ teks). A milky liquid which is used to make rubber.

manioc (man′ ə ok). A plant with large roots from which flour can be made.

navigable (nav′ i gə bəl). Able to be traveled on by ships.

plantation (plan tā′ shən). A large farm or estate on which cotton, tobacco, sugar cane, or other single crops are grown.

sap (sap). The liquid that circulates through a plant.

source (sôrs). The point of origin of a stream of water.

tributary (trib yə terē). A river or stream flowing into a larger river or lake.

vulcanize (vul′ kənīz). To improve rubber by mixing it with sulfur and other things using heat and pressure.

Pronunciation Key: h**a**t, **ā**ge, c**ã**re, f**ä**r; l**e**t, **ē**qual, t**ė**rm; **i**t, **ī**ce; h**o**t, **ō**pen, **ô**rder; **oi**l; **ou**t; c**u**p, p**u̇**t, r**ü**le; **ch**ild; lo**ng**; **th**in; /ͲH/ for **th**en; /zh/ for mea**s**ure; /u/ or /ə/ represents /a/ in **a**bout, /e/ in tak**e**n, /i/ in penc**i**l, /o/ in lem**o**n, and /u/ in circ**u**s.

The World's Largest River System

The Amazon River carries more water than any other river in the world. The Amazon is the world's largest river system. It is not, however, the longest river in the world. The Nile River in North Africa is a little bit longer.

The **source** of the Amazon is in the Andes Mountains of western South America. It flows east from there to the Atlantic Ocean. Most of the huge river and its many tributaries are in the country of Brazil (br ə zil′). There are many places on the Amazon where a person on one side of the river cannot see the other side. The Brazilians call the Amazon the "River Sea." The Amazon is **navigable** from the ocean to Peru. Ocean ships can travel on the Amazon all the way across Brazil, and most of South America, to the city of Iquitos in Peru.

The Amazon River and its tributaries are called the Amazon Basin. There are over 200 of these smaller rivers that flow into the Amazon. The Rio Negro is one important **tributary**.

Its name means "black river." The water of the Rio Negro is clear and black compared to the brown, muddy water of the Amazon. When the Rio Negro flows into the Amazon, its clear water flows side by side with the muddy Amazon water before the two mix together.

Most ocean ships come into the Amazon at the port city of Belém on the Atlantic Ocean. They go up another river to the Amazon and head upstream. One major stop for the ships is the city of Manaus on the Rio Negro. It is 1,000 miles from the mouth of the Amazon. Manaus is a major trading center for the products of the Amazon rainforest. Another one is Iquitos, in Peru, the largest Amazon city.

The Amazon Region

Answer these questions from the map and the text.

2.1   In what direction does the Amazon River flow? _____

2.2   Is the Amazon the longest river in the world? _____

2.3   Name three countries of the Amazon rainforest. _____

_____

2.4   What important Amazon trading centers can be reached by ocean ships?

_____

2.5   What does _Rio Negro_ mean? _____

2.6   What do Brazilians call the Amazon River? _____

2.7   By what port do most ships enter the Amazon? _____

The Amazon Basin is on a very flat plain. The area of tropical rainforest around it is called _selva_. Although there is no winter or summer, there is a wet and a dry season. The wet season is from December to May. A hundred inches of rain may fall in just those few months. The rain makes the river rise and flood the flat land in every direction. The flood waters may go 30 miles in every direction from the river.

The area of the forest that floods every year is called the _várzea_. The part that does not flood is called _terra firma_ (firm ground). Most of the people in Amazonia (the Amazon region) live on the várzea. That is because the mud from the flooded river makes the soil fertile each year, so after the water goes down, the people can grow crops. They have to build their homes on stilts. During the wet season the houses become small islands and the people get around in boats.

During the flood season, the fish swim among the trees of the forest. Many of them eat fruit from the trees. Others eat insects that fall from the trees, or they may jump out of the water and catch the bugs. The fish spread the seeds from the trees, which are inside the fruit, all over the forest. The fish get fat from the abundant food, and many eat little the rest of the year.

There are numerous different species of fish in the Amazon River. The most **infamous** is the piranha. Many piranhas are meat-eating fish with razor-sharp teeth. They rarely attack people, but in a group they can eat a large animal in a matter of minutes. They often take bites of the fins and tails of other fish. Another Amazon fish, the pirarucú, can be 10 feet long and weigh 400 pounds! There are even air-breathing dolphins that live in the Amazon. They can be seen playing among the trees during the flood season.

| Piranha

The sloth is a very unusual animal of the Amazon rainforest. Sloths are very slow-moving animals that hang upside down in the trees. They spend their lives slowly moving along under branches eating leaves. They have hook-like claws on their arms and legs to keep them attached to the trees. They even sleep hanging upside down! Sloths on the ground can only crawl awkwardly. However, when the forest is flooded, they are very good swimmers!

The hoatzin is an unusual Amazon bird. Hoatzin chicks are born with hooks on their wings. They use the hooks to climb around in the trees before they are large enough to fly. Hoatzins can fly only short distances even when they are fully grown. They usually climb. They build their nests over water. If danger threatens, the birds dive into the water. They climb back up the tree after the danger has past.

Like all rainforests, Amazonia has thousands upon thousands of different species of animals. Scientists who work there often discover new species. Some have named and classified hundreds of new species!

| Hoatzin

Match the following.

2.8	_____ *várzea*	a.	slow animals that live upside down
2.9	_____ *selva*	b.	all Amazon tropical rainforest
2.10	_____ *terra firma*	c.	fish, can be 10 ft. long, 400 pounds
2.11	_____ piranha	d.	rainforest that floods
2.12	_____ pirarucú	e.	rainforest that does not flood
2.13	_____ sloth	f.	tree-climbing bird
2.14	_____ hoatzin	g.	meat-eating fish with sharp teeth

Answer these questions.

2.15 What happens to the Amazon during the wet season?

_____

_____

2.16 How do the trees and the fish help each other?

_____

History of Amazonia

Exploration. There were many Indian tribes living in Amazonia before the Age of Exploration brought Europeans to the region. Most of the Amerindians (American Indians) were slash-and-burn farmers who also hunted and gathered. No great cities or governments were built in the Amazon jungle before the Europeans arrived.

Two great European sea nations, Spain and Portugal, were interested in South America. They sent soldiers to conquer the land and take its wealth for themselves. Eventually, Portugal gained control of Brazil, and Spain conquered the rest of the continent.

There was a great nation of people called the Inca who lived in the mountains of Peru above the rainforest. This powerful and wealthy nation was conquered by Francisco

Pizarro of Spain in about 1530. Pizarro's brother, Gonzalo, and Francisco de Orelana set out down the eastern side of the Andes into Amazonia in 1541. They were searching for "El Dorado," a city of gold. It did not exist, but they believed the stories enough to search for it.

The expedition quickly ran into problems in the strange rainforest. The biggest problem was hunger. The men did not know how to find food there. Orelana and some of the men headed down the river to get food for the rest of the group. They were not able to go back up the river and were forced to float down it all the way across the continent. The trip took them eight months.

On the long journey to the sea, the men claimed to have been attacked by a group of fighting women! The ancient Greeks had a story about women warriors called "Amazons." The river Orelana traveled was therefore named the Amazon.

The Portuguese quickly began to send settlers to their new colony to stop Spain from claiming it. They found a tree that produced a valuable red **dye** growing along the coast. The color was *brasa* in Portuguese. The name for the new colony, Brazil, came from these *Brazilwood* trees.

The rainforests of the Amazon were too dangerous and thick for the Portuguese to settle there. They set up a few cities along the river, but settled mostly along the coast to the south of the great river. The city of Manaus was established as a fort in 1660 on the Rio Negro.

For the next two hundred years very little changed in the Amazon. A few Amerindian tribes and settlers lived in the rainforest. Some would bring products from the jungle to the river cities for trade. Brazil nuts, turtle oil, cocoa, fragrant oils, fish, and valuable wood were traded for iron tools and other manufactured items.

Naturalists eventually became interested in the lush forests. They began to explore Amazonia in about the mid 1700s. They came to collect and classify samples of the many species there. One man, Charles Marie de la Condamine, made an important discovery. The Indians showed him a tree whose milky **sap** became elastic when it dried. Condamine took some samples from "the wood that weeps" back to Europe with him. He had discovered rubber.

| Rubber tree sap

Rubber was very useful, but it had a serious problem. It got sticky in the heat and brittle in the cold. In 1839 an American, Charles Goodyear, invented a process called **vulcanizing**. It made rubber strong and useable in any temperature. This invention brought some changes to the Amazon rainforest.

Complete the sentences.

2.17 The river was named after the Amazons, who were _____ _____ from ancient Greek stories.

2.18 Gonzalo Pizarro and a. _____ set out down the east side of the Andes to search for b. _____ in 1541.

2.19 Brazil was named for the a. _____ tree which produced a valuable b. _____ dye.

2.20 "The wood that weeps" produces _____ .

2.21 The two European nations that conquered South America were _____ and _____ .

2.22 Manaus was established as a fort in (year) _____ .

2.23 _____ is the process that makes rubber stronger.

2.24 Some of the products of the rainforest brought in for trade were _____ , _____ , and _____ .

Rubber boom. Once the process of vulcanization was invented, companies began to make many kinds of new rubber products, such as boots and seals for machines. American and European companies began buying large amounts of **latex** from Brazil. This **boom** in Brazilian rubber began around 1870, but it was the need for automobile tires that brought the greatest wealth to the new rubber producers.

Other rainforests had rubber trees, but those in Amazonia were by far the best. However, the trees could not be planted on farms or **plantations** because if they were next to each other, the insects would eat them. Therefore, people had to find the trees in the rainforest, cut slits in them, leave cups to collect the latex, and come back later to get it.

| Manaus Opera House

Thousands of people moved to the rainforest to work collecting rubber. Most of these people were hired by wealthy rubber merchants. The rubber merchants loaned them money to come down the river and buy tools. Each rubber merchant's collectors were forced to sell the rubber only to their rubber merchant at low prices and buy supplies only from them at high prices. That meant the collectors were always in debt to their merchant and could not leave to do something else. This is called *debt slavery*.

The rubber merchants quickly became very rich. The center of the rubber trade was the city of Manaus on the Rio Negro. It became first a boom town and then a beautiful, wealthy city. It had electricity before most of the cities in the United States did! The newly rich merchants built huge expensive homes and brought in new automobiles to travel on the city's few roads. They built a magnificent opera house with crystal chandeliers and decorated tiles brought all the way from Europe!

However, the rubber boom only lasted about forty years, ending by 1913. Some clever men had taken the seeds of the Amazon rubber trees and began growing them in the Asian rainforests. The trees grew well there, and they could be grown on plantations. The insects that could destroy them were in South America!

The new Asian rubber plantations began to produce more and more latex. The price of rubber began to fall as more was being sold. The Amazon merchants could not afford to sell their rubber as cheaply as the Asian merchants. Amazon rubber was much harder to find and collect since it was spread out through the forest. The wealthy merchants lost their money and left. Manaus became once again a small trading town with many beautiful buildings that were slowly overrun by the jungle.

From 1913 to the 1960s, the rainforest was left to the Amerindians, scientists, and a few rubber collectors. Then, the government of Brazil decided it was time to start using the forest.

HISTORY
& GEOGRAPHY 405

LIFEPAC TEST

NAME _____

DATE _____

SCORE _____

HISTORY & GEOGRAPHY 405: LIFEPAC TEST

From the following list write the correct answers in the blanks (2 points each answer).

debt slavery	El Dorado	tropics	canopy
understory	ecotourism	FUNAI	slash and burn
hunter/gatherers		missionaries	

1. The Spanish explored the Amazon when they were looking for

   _____ , the city of gold.

2. _____ is the part of Brazil's government that works with the forest

   Indians.

3. The upper level of the rainforest that is like a huge green roof is called the

   _____ .

4. The rubber collectors in the Amazon were forced to stay at their jobs by

   _____ .

5. Most farming in the rainforest is _____ .

6. The Pygmies are _____ , because they do not plant

   gardens.

7. The dark, middle level of the rainforest is called the _____ .

8. The _____ is the region along both sides of the equator.

9. _____ in the Congo operate some of the working schools and

   hospitals.

10. _____ is a way to keep the rainforests so people can pay to

    come and see them.

Answer these questions.

11. Why could rubber be produced cheaper in Asia than it was in Brazil? (3 points)

    _____

    _____

12. What are the three regions of rainforest in the world? (6 points)

a. _____

b. _____

c. _____

13. What happened in the Congo when Mobutu became dictator in 1965? (4 points)

_____

_____

_____

14. Why is rainforest land not good for crops and cattle ranching? (4 points)

_____

_____

15. How did the Europeans treat the people of Brazil and the Congo after they took control of their land? (3 points)

_____

_____

Write _A_ if the statement is about the Amazon River or rainforest, _C_ if it is about the Congo, and _AC_ if it is true of both (3 points each answer).

16. _____ It was explored by Henry Stanley.

17. _____ The Belgian king made it his own private land.

18. _____ The river is navigable from the ocean almost all the way across the continent.

19. _____ Many, many species of plants and animals live there.

20. _____ The region is wet and hot.

21. _____ The river's source is in the Andes Mountains.

22. _____ Government roads are letting people in to destroy the forest.

23. _____ The region was a colony of Portugal.

24. _____ The flow of water in the river is about the same all year. It does not have a large flood season.

25. _____ Pygmies live there.

Match the following (2 points each answer).

26.	_____ tapir	a.	bird with beautiful feathers
27.	_____ gorilla	b.	sharp-toothed, meat eating fish
28.	_____ piranha	c.	tree-climbing bird
29.	_____ anaconda	d.	eats and lives upside down
30.	_____ sloth	e.	large snake
31.	_____ elephant	f.	intelligent ape, lives only in the Congo
32.	_____ hoatzin		
33.	_____ hippopotamus	g.	largest land animal in the world
34.	_____ pygmy chimpanzee	h.	rhinoceros family, looks like a pig
35.	_____ Bird of Paradise	i.	"river horse"
		j.	large, very shy apes

Answer *true* or *false* (1 point each answer).

36. _____ The Rio Negro is a tributary of the Congo.

37. _____ The Congo rainforest is the largest in the world.

38. _____ The Amazon is the longest river in the world.

39. _____ The Congo River crosses the equator two times.

40. _____ Most of the Amazon Indians farm, as well as gather and hunt in the forest.

41. _____ Kinshasa and Matadi are cities in Brazil.

42. _____ Both the Congo and the Amazon empty into the Atlantic Ocean.

43. _____ Latex is the sap of a tree.

44. _____ Vulcanizing made rubber usable in any temperature.

45. _____ The people of the Congo belong to different tribes that often do not trust each other.

Complete the sentences.

2.25   The Brazilian rubber boom lasted from _____ to _____ .

2.26   The rubber collectors were forced to stay on the job by being held in

_____ .

2.27   The center of the rubber boom was the city of _____ .

2.28   The need for _____ for automobiles greatly increased the need for latex.

Answer this question.

2.29   Why could the Asian rubber merchants sell more latex at a cheaper price?

_____

_____

_____

Opening the Amazon. The government of Brazil decided in the 1960s to start building roads into Amazonia. They wanted to begin making money from this region of their nation. In 1966 the government began "Operation Amazonia." The operation was supposed to settle 100,000 poor families in farming villages along newly-created roads, but the poor soil would not grow crops for long, and the project failed.

Still, by 1970 the government had built ten times as many miles of road as there had been in 1966. The longest road they built was the Trans-Amazon Highway which cuts through the rainforest from the Atlantic Ocean west across the entire country.

As the new roads were built, thousands of people came hoping to get land for themselves. Many were given land by the government. Others simply took an empty place and started clearing it.

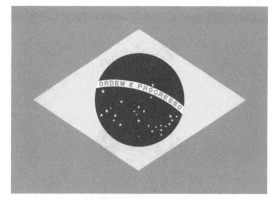

| Flag of Brazil

Worse yet for the rainforest, the government sold large areas to wealthy people for cattle ranches. The land was cleared in huge sections for the cattle.

Large companies began mining for iron and other important metals in the forest. Gold was discovered in several places. This created gold rushes, as men came to the area to try to become rich. These people destroyed the forest and polluted the river as they dug for minerals.

The land cleared by all of these people quickly became worthless, almost desert land. But Brazil owes such a huge amount of money to other countries that it is willing to destroy the future use of the land for money to pay debts today. Many countries around the world are trying to encourage Brazil to save its forests. So far, little is changing.

The future. Many scientists are experimenting to find ways for people to earn money from the rainforest without destroying it. They are trying to find crops that will grow in the forest and provide money for families that live there. They are finding new ways to use forest plants so that they can be harvested and sold.

Ecotourism is one way of making money without destroying the forest and it is slowly becoming more popular. People who like to see the rainforest come and pay money to visit. The people who live in the forest can guide them around and sell them supplies or crafts. There are several companies that arrange these kinds of vacations. In one place a bridge was even put up high in the trees so these visitors can look at the plants and animals in the canopy. Hopefully, new ideas may one day solve the problem so that the Amazon rainforest will stop being destroyed.

| Bridge above rainforest

Answer *true* or *false*.

2.30 _____ Brazil owes other countries a large amount of money.

2.31 _____ Cattle ranchers make useless rainforest into fertile, productive land.

2.32 _____ Brazil began building more roads into Amazonia in the 1960s.

2.33 _____ No important metals can be found in the forest.

2.34 _____ "Operation Amazonia" was supposed to preserve large parts of the forest as national parks.

2.35 _____ The Trans-Amazon Highway was never finished.

2.36 _____ No one is interested in ecotourism.

Amerindians of the Amazon

The early Portuguese settlers were very cruel to the Indians. They killed them or took them as slaves. Many died of European diseases like measles and smallpox. Some of the Catholic priests who came with the settlers (Portugal is a Catholic nation) tried to protect the Indians. They built villages where they could come to live, learn the Catholic faith, and be taught a useful trade. But outside the villages, many of the Indians died of overwork, murder, and disease. Within a hundred years after the arrival of the Portuguese, probably two-thirds of the Indians had died.

The tribes deep in the selva were protected by the dense forest for many years. They lived their lives in a traditional manner without any outside contact. They were all slash-and-burn farmers who also hunted and gathered from the forest. They moved their villages after a number of years either to clear new gardens or to escape enemy tribes.

Each of the about 200 Amazon tribes had its own culture. Many of them fought each other. Some, like the Yanomami, also spelled Yanomamö or Yanomama, fought constantly. Perhaps one out of every four Yanomami men died in a fight of some sort! All the Indians believed in evil spirits that live in the land, plants, and animals.

The Indians had many clever ways of getting food from the forest. In their gardens they usually grew **manioc** as their main food. It is a root which they ground into a type of flour.

They also grew banana and palm trees for their fruit. If they wanted fish, they could hunt for them with a harpoon or net. Sometimes they would dam up a part of a stream and spread poison from a tree in the water. The fish in the stream could then be picked up by hand when they floated to the top.

| Bananas are a common export of the Amazon region.

The white settlers and rubber collectors in the forest were just as cruel to the Indians as the Portuguese had been. In 1910 the government of Brazil created an organization to protect the Indians. It was led by Marechal Candido Rondon and was called the Service for the Protection of Indians (SPI). Rondon worked hard to make peaceful contact with the forest tribes and prepare them to face the modern world. He wanted to make sure their land was protected and would not be taken away from them.

After Rondon's death, the SPI began to help wealthy landowners kill the Indians and take their land. The SPI was disbanded in 1968, and a new government group, FUNAI, was set up to protect the Indians. The new organization has tried to set up protected areas where the Indians can safely live in the forest, but many of the tribes are dying of diseases as they come into more contact with Brazilians and outsiders. Often their land is taken for road and dam projects. Even more often, settlers just move into Indian land and start clearing it or mining for gold. The government often does not stop them and, in some cases, even helps the settlers.

Many people are trying to help the Indians. Some in the government try to pass laws and make the people obey them. Some of the people in FUNAI work hard to help the Indians become part of the modern world. People who want to protect the rainforest want large parts of it to be given to the Indians for their home. Many of the Indians have begun organizing into groups to argue with the government and the settlers. Some of the Indians have even kidnapped government officials to make the government better protect their land.

Missionaries have worked in the Amazon for many, many years. They bring medicine to treat the diseases brought by the white people, which continue to kill hundreds of Indians. They also teach the Indians to read and write so they can work to protect themselves.

Missionary groups bring airplanes into the jungle to fly people out in emergencies and to supply the missions.

Many **anthropologists** do not like the Christian missionaries in spite of the good work they do. The anthropologists say the missionaries are destroying the Indians' culture by teaching them about Jesus. Becoming Christian does change the Indians' culture by stopping their worship of spirits and many of the cruel things they used to do. Many other changes are coming into their culture as they learn some of the ways of the white settlers. Their cultures are being changed no matter what anyone does to stop it. The missionaries want to be sure that they know about Jesus as they face the difficult changes ahead of them.

Complete the sentences.

2.37   The government group that was set up to protect the Indians in 1968 was

_____ .

2.38   The Portuguese were _____ to the Indians.

2.39   Many Indians continue to die from _____ .

2.40   Many anthropologists do not think that the missionaries should do anything

that might change the Indians' _____ .

2.41   The Indians today are trying to protect their _____ from settlers.

Answer these questions.

2.42   Who started SPI and what did it try to do?

_____

_____

_____

2.43   What do the missionaries do to help the Indians?

_____

_____

_____

2.44   What is the traditional way of life of the forest Indians?

_____

_____

_____

Review the material in this section to prepare for the Self Test. The Self Test will check your understanding of this section and the previous section. Any items you miss on this test will show you what areas you will need to restudy in order to prepare for the unit test.

SELF TEST 2

Match the following (3 points each answer).

2.01	_____	Amazon	a.	Amazon forest that does not flood
2.02	_____	Manaus	b.	black-colored Amazon tributary
2.03	_____	Rio Negro	c.	longest river in the world
2.04	_____	the Andes	d.	most of Amazonia is in this nation
2.05	_____	Brazil	e.	mountains of South America
2.06	_____	Portugal	f.	named for Greek stories of women warriors
2.07	_____	*selva*		
2.08	_____	*terra firma*	g.	most tropical rainforests are near it
2.09	_____	Nile	h.	European nation that conquered Brazil
2.010	_____	equator		
			i.	center of the rubber boom
			j.	Amazon rainforest

Answer these questions.

2.011 What are the three layers of the rainforest? (2 points each answer)

a. _____

b. _____

c. _____

2.012 What happens to the *várzea* during the wet season? (2 points this answer)

_____

2.013 Why did the Asian rubber merchants put the Brazilians out of business? (4 points this answer)

_____

_____

_____

2.014 Why is rainforest land not good for crops and cattle? (4 points this answer)

_____

_____

_____

2.015 Where are the three major regions of tropical rainforests in the world?
(2 points each answer)

a. _____

b. _____

c. _____

Choose the correct answer from the list below (3 points each answer).

piranha	sloth	anaconda	debt slavery
hoatzin	latex	FUNAI	ecotourism
orchids	El Dorado		

2.016 _____ is the government group in Brazil that works to help the Indians.

2.017 Many rubber collectors were held at their jobs by _____ .

2.018 The _____ slowly eats its way along, upside down in the trees.

2.019 The _____ is a tree-climbing bird because it cannot fly well.

2.020 People who encourage _____ say that travelers will pay to see the rainforest left as it is.

2.021 Rubber is made from the _____ of the rubber tree.

2.022 The _____ is a feared fish of the Amazon River.

2.023 The _____ is a large snake that squeezes its prey to death.

2.024 _____ are a type of air plant that does not need soil.

2.025 Francisco de Orelana was searching for _____ when he explored the Amazon River.

Answer *true* or *false* (2 points each answer).

2.026 _____ Many Indians died of cruel treatment and disease after the Portuguese came to the Amazon.

2.027 _____ Most of the Indians were hunter/gatherers who did not do any kind of farming.

2.028 _____ Brazil is trying to protect the rainforest and make most of it into a national park.

2.029 _____ Marechal Candido Rondon, who led the SPI, tried to make peaceful contact with the forest Indian tribes.

2.030 _____ "Operation Amazonia" was intended to settle many poor families on farms in the rainforest.

2.031 _____ Rainforests have only a few kinds of trees and animals.

2.032 _____ Rubber that is not vulcanized becomes sticky in the heat and brittle in the cold.

2.033 _____ The Trans-Amazon Highway goes all the way across Amazonia in Brazil from east to west.

2.034 _____ Brazil owes other countries a great deal of money.

Teacher check:

Score _____

Initials _____

Date _____

80
100

3. THE CONGO RAINFOREST

The rainforest of Central Africa runs across six nations: Cameroon, Central African Republic, Republic of the Congo, Democratic Republic of the Congo, Gabon, and Equatorial Guinea. The Congo River flows through the center of this rainforest. The river and one of its major tributaries form the border between the Democratic Republic of the Congo (DR Congo, DRC) and another country the Republic of the Congo (Congo Rep.) and the Central African Republic.

You will learn in this section about this river and its history. You will also learn about the nation of Congo as well as the people and the animals of the Congo forest.

Objectives

Review these objectives. When you have completed this section, you should be able to:

1. Describe rainforests and tell where they are located.
2. Name some of the products of the rainforest.
3. Identify some of the rainforest plants and animals.
4. Explain the history of the Amazon and Congo rainforests.
5. Describe the Congo and Amazon Rivers.
6. Tell of the changes being made in the rainforest.
7. Describe how people live in the rainforest.

Vocabulary

Study these new words. Learning the meanings of these words is a good study habit and will improve your understanding of this LIFEPAC.

antelope (an' tə lōp). An animal of Africa and Asia that chews its cud and has hoofs.

ape (āp). A large, tailless monkey with long arms. Apes can stand almost erect and walk on two feet.

bribe (brīb). Anything given to get someone to do something wrong.

civil war (siv' əl wôr). A war between people from the same country.

dictator (dik' tā tor). A person who rules and has total power over the government.

dugout (dug' out'). A boat made by hollowing out a large log.

endangered (en dān' jərd). Something that may stop existing.

ivory (ī' vər ē). A hard, white material; elephants' tusks.

plantain (plan' tin). A kind of large banana.

rapids (rap' ids). A part of a river where the water rushes quickly, often over rocks lying near the surface.

Pronunciation Key: hat, āge, cãre, fär; let, ēqual, tėrm; it, īce; hot, ōpen, ôrder; oil; out; cup, pu̇t, rüle; child; long; thin; /ŦH/ for then; /zh/ for measure; /u/ or /ə/ represents /a/ in about, /e/ in taken, /i/ in pencil, /o/ in lemon, and /u/ in circus.

The Congo River

The Congo River in central Africa is one of the longest rivers in the world. It is over 2,700 miles long, making it the second-largest river system in the world. Only the Amazon River carries more water. The river's source is in the mountains of the Great Rift Valley, which runs down the eastern side of Africa. The river flows in a bow shape. It starts in southern Congo and flows north, then, it turns in a curve to go west and south to the ocean.

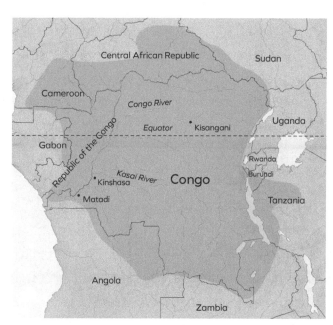

| The Democratic Republic of the Congo (also known as Congo) and its neighbors

The Congo River crosses the equator <u>twice</u> on its way to the Atlantic Ocean. The river and its tributaries get water from both sides of the equator. The wet and dry seasons come at different times on the two sides, so the Congo does not have a heavy flood every year like the Amazon. When the northern tributaries are in the wet season, the southern ones are not. Therefore, the flow of water in the river is about the same all year.

Also unlike the Amazon, the Congo has several areas of **rapids** and waterfalls that ships cannot pass. This means that ocean ships cannot use the river to carry goods into Congo. Ships can travel in many places in between the rapids, however. About 9,000 miles of the river and its tributaries can be used by riverboats to trade between the towns and cities of the Congo.

| Waterfalls near Kiubo Falls village, Democratic Republic of Congo

Ships from the ocean can only sail up the river to the city of Matadi, about 90 miles from the mouth. Between Matadi and Kinshasa, the capital of Congo, there are <u>thirty</u> different waterfalls that no ship can sail through.

The capital is built above the waterfalls, where the river forms a lake called Pool Malebo. Beyond Kinshasa, ships can safely sail and carry goods all the way to Kisangani. Above Kisangani is yet another group of waterfalls. These are called Wagenia Falls. The capital is built above the waterfalls, where the river forms a lake called Pool Malebo. Beyond Kinshasa, ships can safely sail and carry goods all the way to Kisangani. Above Kisangani is yet another group of waterfalls. These are called Wagenia Falls. Above the falls, the Congo River is called the Lualaba River. The river has this name from its source in the mountains to the Wagenia Falls.

Do these map activities.

3.1   The Congo River crosses the _____ (map line) twice.

3.2   Name five rainforest nations of Central Africa.

a. _____

b. _____

c. _____

d. _____

e. _____

3.3   The Congo River is called the _____ River at its source.

3.4   Name three major cities on the Congo River.

a. _____

b. _____

c. _____

3.5   The capital of Congo is on a lake called Pool _____ .

3.6   The mouth of the Congo River is on the _____ Ocean.

Answer *true* or *false*.

3.7   _____   Both the Amazon and the Congo have a large flood season each
year.

3.8   _____   The Congo River's source is in the mountains of the Great Rift Valley.

3.9   _____   The Congo carries more water than the Amazon.

3.10   _____   The Congo is navigable from its mouth to almost its source.

Tropical rainforest covers most of the northern part of the Congo. This forest and its river were the subject of a famous book called *The Heart of Darkness* by Joseph Conrad. The name is a good description of the dark, thick forest of central Africa. This forest continues to be a wild, untamed place. Hunting has **endangered** many of the animals there, but the jungle itself is not being destroyed as it is in Brazil.

Like all rainforests, the Congo Basin is home to many unusual animals and plants. The pygmy chimpanzee, for example, lives only in the Congo rainforests. Chimpanzees are the most intelligent of the **apes**. They live together in groups and eat many different kinds of food. Sometimes they will hunt and kill smaller animals to eat. The groups spend time every day combing each other's fur with their fingers, cleaning out any dirt, leaves, or bugs they find. The pygmy chimps are smaller than the other kinds of chimpanzees. They tend to climb in the trees more than other chimps. They are more like monkeys that way.

The hippopotamus is another animal that can be found in the Congo rainforest, usually in the river. Its name comes from the Greek words for "river horse." These huge animals can grow to be 15 feet long and weigh 3,000 pounds! They swim very well and can actually walk along the bottom of the river! They usually stay in the water during the day and come out to eat grass or leaves at night. The people of the Congo love to eat hippopotamus meat. Many of the hippos are killed for food, even though it is illegal.

African elephants also live in the rainforest. Elephants are the largest land animals in the world. Male African elephants grow to be about 11 feet tall at the shoulder and weigh about 12,000 pounds. Elephants are vegetarians (eat only plants). They can eat over 750 pounds of food in a day! Elephants use their trunks to gather food and water. The end of this long nose can pick up something as small as a coin or a peanut.

African elephants have long teeth called tusks that stick out from the sides of their mouths. These tusks are made of **ivory**. Elephants have been hunted for years for their valuable tusks. In the 1970s and 80s, thousands of elephants were killed using modern rifles. The valuable tusks were worth more than several months' pay to the poor people of central Africa. This has made elephants an endangered species, because so many have been killed.

| Elephant

In 1989, a group from the United Nations ordered all selling of new ivory stopped. This has helped the elephants somewhat.

Gorillas also live in the rainforest of central Africa. The gorillas of the Congo rainforest are called *lowland gorillas*. Gorillas are the largest of the apes. A male gorilla may weigh 450 pounds and stand 6 feet tall on its hind legs. In spite of their huge size, gorillas are very shy creatures. They will not attack anyone if they are left alone. They live in groups led by an adult male and eat plants. Their only enemies are people, who kill them and destroy the forests they need to survive.

| Gorilla

Write the letter of the correct animal in each blank.

3.11	_____ largest of the apes	a.	gorilla
3.12	_____ largest land animal	b.	hippopotamus
3.13	_____ "river horse"	c.	pygmy chimpanzee
3.14	_____ large animals, live in groups, eat plants, shy	d.	elephant
3.15	_____ most intelligent of the apes		
3.16	_____ live only in the rainforests of Congo		
3.17	_____ killed for their ivory tusks		
3.18	_____ stay in the river in the day, come out to eat at night		
3.19	_____ use their fingers to comb each other's fur		
3.20	_____ can eat 750 pounds of food in a day		

History of the Congo

There were several important kingdoms in the Congo region before the Europeans came there. The Kongo Empire was one of these. The Kongo was a group of small states near the mouth of the Congo River ruled by a king. That nation gave the river its name.

The Portuguese came to the Kongo for the first time in the 1480s. Portugal was sailing farther and farther along the coast of Africa to reach India and China on the other side. At first they made friends with the Kongo nation. They sent missionaries and ambassadors. Unfortunately, the friendship did not last. The Portuguese were more interested in making money than making friends.

It is especially sad that the Portuguese treated the people of the Kongo so badly. The king of Kongo became a Christian and took the name Afonso. He wanted to learn from the Europeans and teach his people, but the Portuguese only wanted to use their friendship with Afonso to gain slaves to sell. Many people were sold as slaves, and within 100 years the kingdom of Kongo was destroyed.

The Portuguese could not sail up the river because of the waterfalls near the mouth. Also, the humid, tropical region was uncomfortable and unhealthy for Europeans. So, the Congo area was not explored or claimed again by any European country for many years.

In the 1870s one of the most famous missionary/explorers in history, Dr. David Livingstone, was living in central Africa. (He had explored the Zambezi River in East Africa.) No one had seen him since he began his trip in 1865. A New York newspaper sent a reporter named Henry Stanley to find the great man. Stanley found Livingstone near Lake Tanganyika (on the border of Tanzania and the Congo) in 1871. Stanley was very impressed by the elderly man of God and afterward began to explore Africa himself.

| Stanley and Livingstone meet in an African village.

Stanley became the first man known to have followed the Congo River across Africa to its mouth. He proved that there were many miles of navigable river above the waterfalls.

His discoveries interested King Leopold of Belgium. The king hired him to build a road around the waterfalls and trading posts along the river itself. In this way, the king gained control of the river basin. In 1885, Leopold used his control of the river to claim all of the Congo as his own private land!

The region was named the Congo Free State, but it was not free. King Leopold only cared about making money from the land. The people were treated very cruelly. They were forced into slavery to build roads and gather rubber latex. When they did not do what their Belgian masters wanted, they were often killed. Missionaries in the Congo began to write letters and articles about the awful things that were happening. Joseph Conrad's book, *The Heart of Darkness*, was written about this horrible period of time.

Eventually the anger over what was happening forced the government of Belgium to take the land away from the king. It was renamed the Belgian Congo, but Belgium did not do very much to help the people. Catholic missionaries did set up schools, with help from the government. But Europeans ran all the schools, businesses, army, large farms, and government.

Before World War II (1939–1945), almost all the countries of Africa were European colonies. After the war, these nations began to demand and receive their independence. Belgium did not want to give the Congo its independence, but after a riot in 1958, they made an agreement. The Congo became a free nation in June of 1960.

Answer *true* or *false*.

3.21 _____ Before World War II, almost all the countries of Africa were colonies of Europe.

3.22 _____ Henry Stanley was the first man to travel down the length of the Congo River.

3.23 _____ King Leopold treated the Congo people kindly.

3.24 _____ Dr. Livingstone was a famous scientist.

3.25 _____ King Afonso was an African Christian who wanted to learn from the Europeans.

3.26 _____ The Belgian government took the Congo away from King Leopold.

3.27 _____ The Portuguese were only interested in getting slaves, not friendship, from the Kongo Empire.

3.28 _____ Henry Stanley set up trading posts on the Congo River for the king of England.

3.29 _____ The Belgians were the first Europeans to visit the Kongo Empire.

 Do this activity.

3.30 Write a one-act play on the meeting of reporter Henry Stanley from the New York newspaper and Dr. Livingstone, the missionary. You may work with a friend. Check an encyclopedia or do research online for information about how it happened. The time will be November 10, 1871. The place will be an African village. Ask your teacher if you can read your play to the class or perform it.

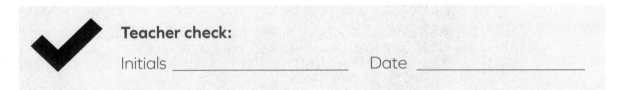

Teacher check:

Initials _____ Date _____

The people of Congo do not think of themselves as being from one nation. They belong to about 250 different tribes or groups. Each has its own language and culture. The Belgians forced these people to become part of one country. They often do not trust each other. They did not trust each other when the Republic of the Congo (its name then) was formed in 1960.

A few days after independence, the army rebelled and the Congo was divided by a **civil war**. The war finally ended in 1964 when men from European armies were hired to fight for the government. Even after the war, the government was not able to end all the fighting and disagreements between the people of the different tribes. In 1965, the head of the army, Joseph Mobutu, took over the government and made himself **dictator**. He changed the name of the country from Congo to Zaïre in 1971.

| Flag of the Democratic Republic of the Congo

Between 1965 and 1997 Mobutu made himself rich and ruined the people of his country. He took the businesses away from their European owners and gave them to his friends. His friends did not run the businesses, they just sold off whatever they could to make money fast. The businesses closed and people lost their jobs. Mobutu began stealing all the money he could and the people in his government did the same.

It was all the stealing that destroyed the country. The roads were not fixed because the money to do it had been stolen. The same was true of the railroads, buses, buildings, and boats. Policemen and soldiers were not paid, so they stole from people and took **bribes**. Doctors and teachers did not get paid for months, because someone had stolen their wages rather than paying them. So, the hospitals and schools would only help people who could pay for these services. There were very few jobs because businesses could not get what they needed to make products; it had all been stolen. By 1997, Congo was one of the poorest and most dangerous places in the world.

Finally, in 1997, Mobutu was driven out of the country by an army of his enemies. They renamed the country the *Democratic Republic of the Congo*. But, after Mobutu left, Laurent Kabila took over as dictator (as of 1997). Only time will tell if things will change.

Within the country, some people are trying to help. The Catholic Church is very large and important in the Congo. The leaders of the church have tried for years to make the government stop stealing. They have run schools and hospitals for the people, because the government ones have no money. The Christian missionaries also work hard to help the people. They use the money sent from outside the country to help the sick and teach the children. The Christian schools and hospitals are often the only ones open.

The awful government has been both good and bad for the rainforest. Without government roads, people cannot get into the rainforest to cut it down, so the forests of the Congo have not been destroyed like those in Brazil. Similar to the tropical forests of the Amazon, the soils of the Congo Basin forests are generally poor in nutrients. Any nutrients made by decaying plants and animals are quickly absorbed by the living plants. When the trees and plants that hold the soil together are removed for farming the soil falls apart and becomes useless. The native people shift their farming from one place to another to find fertile soil. The lack of roads has slowed the clearing of large areas of the rainforest. But the government also does nothing to protect the endangered forest animals from hungry or greedy hunters, so the animals are being destroyed, even if the forest is not.

Answer these questions.

3.31   What happened a few days after the Congo became independent?

_____

3.32   How has the poor government been good for the rainforest?

_____

3.33   How has the bad government been bad for the rainforest?

_____

3.34   Who runs most of the hospitals and schools that are open?

_____

3.35   Who took over the government as dictator in 1965?

_____

3.36   What happened in the Congo under Mobutu that ruined the country?

_____

3.37   Why don't the people of Congo think of themselves as a nation?

_____

People of the Congo Rainforest

Most of the tribes in the Congo are from a group called the Bantu. Their families are very important to them. Grandparents, aunts, uncles, and cousins are part of the family. Even a third or fourth cousin is welcomed in their homes if he needs a place to stay.

The homes of the rainforest people are usually made of baked mud. The roofs are covered with leaves. They have a steep slope so that the heavy rains will run off quickly. A person with a good job might have a metal roof. In the cities, however, the people live in houses and apartments just like ours, if they have enough money.

Most Congolese live by farming a small piece of land and hunting or fishing. They farm without machines and usually grow just enough food to stay alive. The roads are so poor that only people that live along the river or very near a city can sell extra food for goods from the city. It often is too far to carry food by walking, for it quickly spoils in the tropical heat.

Most families eat vegetables, bananas, manioc, fish, some meat, and **plantains**. Plantains are a kind of large green banana. These plantains are not eaten raw. When they are roasted, they are a favorite breakfast food. A kind of palm oil is poured over the food for seasoning.

The men who live near Wagenia Falls have a very clever way to trap fish in the river. They build large basket traps that are shaped like a funnel, except the bottom end is closed off. They lower the baskets into the waterfalls from poles they have put up over the river. The fast-moving water goes through the basket, trapping the fish that are there. The fish cannot swim back to the opening of the trap because the water is coming in too quickly.

| Bantu man and woman carrying fruit on their heads.

People who live along the rivers can sell some of their extra food to merchants on the riverboats. The riverboats take people and products between the cities on the Congo. The boats also carry merchants with goods from the city to sell. The people on the rivers paddle hard in **dugout** canoes to meet the slow-moving boats as they come by. Then they tie up to the boat and travel with it for a while as they do their trading. The merchants take the food they buy from the river people back to the city to sell.

Most of the people of Congo belong to a Christian Church. The largest church is the Catholic Church. Almost half the people are Catholic.(Belgium is a Catholic nation, and that church was brought in by them.) The schools run by the Catholic church have done a very good job of teaching the people to read and write. In spite of the trouble in the country, almost three out of four people can read and write. That is very high for Africa. The people of Congo believe education is highly important, even in times of much trouble.

Complete the sentences.

3.38   The largest church is the _____ Church.

3.39   Most people's homes are made of _____ with _____ for the roof.

3.40   People along the river can trade with merchants on the _____ .

3.41   Most of the people can read and write because of the schools run by the _____ .

3.42   Most of the people of the Congo come from the _____ group of people.

3.43   Congolese people usually live by _____

_____ .

3.44   The fishermen of Wagenia Falls use _____ to trap fish in the waterfalls.

3.45   Two things that Congolese eat that Americans usually do not are _____ and _____ .

Deep in the rainforest of the Congo lives a race of short hunter/gatherers. The men are only four feet, six inches (137 centimeters) tall, and the women are even shorter. Because of their small size, outsiders named the people *Pygmies*. They have different names for themselves, depending on where they live. Some of the Congolese pygmies are the Efe and the Mbuti.

Most of the Pygmies live in groups of less than a hundred. They eat foods gathered in the forest. They do not plant gardens. They eat berries, nuts, fruit, fish, and insects (termites are a favorite!). The men are great hunters.

They kill monkeys, **antelope**, birds, and even elephants! Honey taken from bee hives high in the canopy is a special, favorite food. The pygmies may climb over a hundred feet up a tree to reach this treat.

| Baka Pygmy collecting honey

The Pygmies often use nets for hunting. Women and children go along to help. When the hunters see movement among the leaves, they spread their long nets into a half circle. The women and children walk toward the net making loud noises. The loud noises usually frighten nearby animals into the net. The hunters close in on the animals and shoot. Then the meat is shared by all. If no animal is caught, they eat just the forest plants the women have gathered.

Pygmies also catch fish. They sometimes use a natural poison in the rivers, like the Indians of the Amazon to catch fish. Or they may dam up a stream, then gather the fish after the water has gone down.

The pygmies have traded with farming tribes that live in the forest for a long time. The pygmies trade meat and forest fruit for manioc, pots, or metal tools. Pygmies will also work in the gardens in exchange for food or tools. They sometime trade for cloth, too; but, they also will make their own cloth from the bark of trees.

The Pygmies move often. The men go on ahead and find a new location for their camp. The women follow and build new huts. Young trees are cut for the sides of the house and are tied together at the top with strong vines. Wide leaves, sixteen inches (40 centimeters) long, are used to cover the frame. The leaves overlap each other. If the house leaks, more leaves are added. Their cooking fire is outside the hut.

Pygmies do not have leaders or a government. They make decisions together. Everyone in the group is part of the family. Children call all of the adults "mother" or "father."

Today the pygmies are often visited by tourists interested in their way of life. They will charge the tourists to see their villages and dances. They will also take them on walks or hunts in the forest for a fee. However, most of the pygmies still survive by living off the food of the forest.

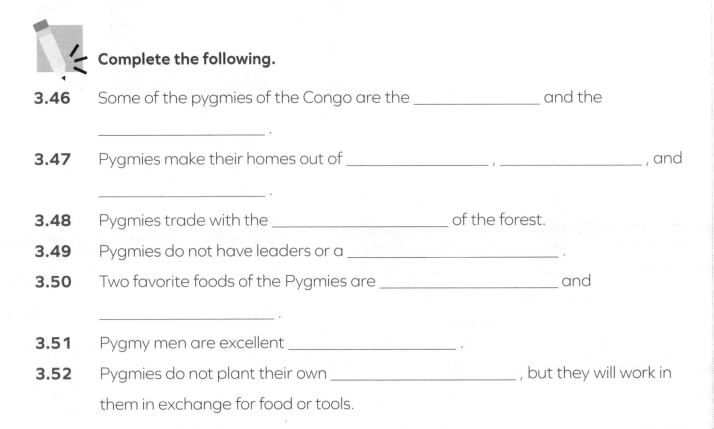

Complete the following.

3.46   Some of the pygmies of the Congo are the _____ and the

_____ .

3.47   Pygmies make their homes out of _____ , _____ , and

_____ .

3.48   Pygmies trade with the _____ of the forest.

3.49   Pygmies do not have leaders or a _____ .

3.50   Two favorite foods of the Pygmies are _____ and

_____ .

3.51   Pygmy men are excellent _____ .

3.52   Pygmies do not plant their own _____ , but they will work in

them in exchange for food or tools.

Do this graph study.

3.53 Sometimes information can be given without using many words. A group of wide lines called a bar graph can show you the lengths of the great rivers of the world. Read the following bar graph and answer the questions.

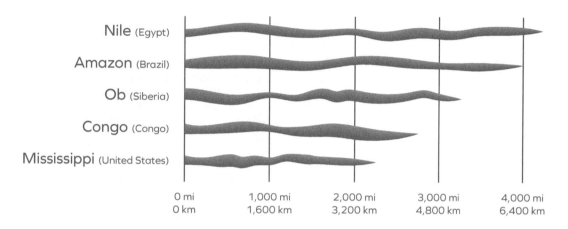

	0 mi	1,000 mi	2,000 mi	3,000 mi	4,000 mi
	0 km	1,600 km	3,200 km	4,800 km	6,400 km

a. What is the longest river on the graph? _____

b. What is the second longest river? _____

c. What is the length of the Nile River? _____

 Before you take this last Self Test, you may want to do one or more of these self checks.

1. _____ Read the objectives. See if you can do them.

2. _____ Restudy the material related to any objectives that you cannot do.

3. _____ Use the **SQ3R** study procedure to review the material:

    a. **S**can the sections.

    b. **Q**uestion yourself.

    c. **R**ead to answer your questions.

    d. **R**ecite the answers to yourself.

    e. **R**eview areas you did not understand.

4. _____ Review all vocabulary, activities, and Self Tests, writing a correct answer for every wrong answer.

SELF TEST 3

Write *A* if the statement is about the Amazon River or rainforest, *C* if it is about the Congo, and *AC* if it is true of both (3 points each answer).

3.01 _____ The forest is always green.

3.02 _____ The forest near the river is flooded for miles every year.

3.03 _____ The river crosses the equator two times.

3.04 _____ It was named for women warriors in Greek stories.

3.05 _____ Rapids and waterfalls block ocean ships from traveling very far up the river.

3.06 _____ The soil is very poor. It gets its nutrients from the dying plants and animals of the forest.

3.07 _____ Rubber was first discovered here and for a short time was an unbelievably valuable product of the forest.

3.08 _____ Kinshasa, Matadi, and Kisangani are cities on the river.

3.09 _____ The river flows east from the Andes Mountains.

3.010 _____ The river empties into the Atlantic Ocean.

Match the following (2 points each answer).

3.011 _____ gorilla

3.012 _____ piranha

3.013 _____ sloth

3.014 _____ hippopotamus

3.015 _____ elephant

3.016 _____ orchid

3.017 _____ manioc

3.018 _____ latex

3.019 _____ pygmy chimpanzee

3.020 _____ anaconda

a. slow-moving, upside-down eating animal of the Amazon

b. "river horse" of Africa

c. sap of the rubber tree

d. hunted for its ivory tusks

e. food plant

f. air plant

g. largest of the apes

h. intelligent ape found only in Congo

i. large snake

j. meat-eating fish with sharp teeth

Write *B* if the statement is about the history of Brazil, *C* if it is about Congo (2 points each answer).

3.021 _____ It was a colony of Belgium.

3.022 _____ It was a colony of Portugal.

3.023 _____ There were several important kingdoms in the area before the arrival of the Europeans.

3.024 _____ The entire country was once the private land of a European king.

3.025 _____ Stealing has destroyed the country.

3.026 _____ The government has built many roads into the forest, which people use to come in and destroy it.

3.027 _____ The river was explored by Henry Stanley, who also set up trading posts.

3.028 _____ The river was first explored by Francisco de Orelana, who was looking for "El Dorado."

3.029 _____ Manaus was established in 1660 as a fort.

3.030 _____ The country got its name from the wood of a tree that produced a valuable red dye.

Answer these questions in complete sentences (4 points each answer).

3.031 What happened in the Congo when it became independent?

_____

3.032 Most of the schools and hospitals in the Congo that are open are run by whom?

_____

3.033 How can people who live along the Congo River get goods from the city?

_____

3.034 Where do pygmies get their food, and what kinds of things do they eat?

_____

_____

_____

Answer *true* or *false* (2 points each answer).

3.035 _____ Congo was named Zaïre under Joseph Mobutu.

3.036 _____ The Portuguese were the first Europeans to visit the Congo region.

3.037 _____ Joseph Mobutu was elected president of the Congo at independence and was a good leader.

3.038 _____ Pygmies do not have any government.

3.039 _____ Most of the people of the Congo are Muslims.

3.040 _____ The rainforests in the Congo and Brazil are being destroyed equally as much.

3.041 _____ The people of Congo belong to over 200 different cultures or tribes.

Teacher check:

Score _____

Initials _____

Date _____

80
___
100

Before you take the LIFEPAC Test, you may want to do one or more of these self checks.

1. _____ Read the objectives. See if you can do them.
2. _____ Restudy the material related to any objectives that you cannot do.
3. _____ Use the **SQ3R** study procedure to review the material.
4. _____ Review activities, Self Tests, and LIFEPAC vocabulary words.
5. _____ Restudy areas of weakness indicated by the last Self Test.

NOTES